AF060454

# West Bound Land Company and Dream Corporation

Mark Fleming Stonesifer
Alecia Zoe Witt Stonesifer

**West Bound Land Company and Dream Corporation**

Printed in the United States of America

Copyright © 2020 Mark Stonesifer and Alecia Zoe Witt Stonesifer
All Rights Reserved

No part of this book may be reproduced in any manner
in any media, or transmitted by any means whatsoever, electronic
or mechanical (including photocopy, film or video recording,
internet posting, or any other information storage and retrieval
system), without the prior written permission of the author.

*To my niece, Cassandra... your world you are growing up in is so different from the one I grew up in, but you possess great gifts and promise for the future. Keep you well updated on local events and your intellectual hunger and genius could light the way for many. I wish you well and good fortune.*

*Your Uncle Mark Stonesifer*

# Contents

| | |
|---|---|
| Down, Way Down | 1 |
| Mr. Mayor | 2 |
| The Angel | 3 |
| Final Testimony | 4 |
| Haiku | 6 |
| Old Times Rocknroll Rhymes | 7 |
| Blue Crab | 8 |
| Rapnroll 2020 | 9 |
| Ra and the Snow Moon Pack | 10 |
| Five Meaningful Haikus Valentine's 2020 | 12 |
| Double Down on St. John's | 13 |
| Here and Now in Tucson | 14 |
| The Best in the West Time Tripper | 15 |
| About the Authors | 17 |

# Down, Way Down

Down, way down
I brought a truck load of weed,
Into my little Texas town
In the Rio grande valley

It was twenty years ago
But somebody done snitched
And into the Paddy wagon and
    County jail I was pitched.

Inside I was given an attorney
Who worked for my handlers.
A year and a half in County
I kept my silence like a gambler

That was twenty years ago,
What they truck in now is surely evil
And now it's hasta luego
Fentynal and meth, all evil.

In another year I retire
19 circuits on the Force
I think about the Border fire
Trying to save families of course

# Mr. Mayor

In writing rhymes I must confess,
Many ideas on life I profess,
I have had limited success,
In doing so my life is not so much a mess.

I had written in the East,
Where my family had a Moveable Feast.
Decided to move out to Tucson in the West,
Where God and the Sun purify the best.

Now I am sitting here in the Sun
Thinking of Mayor Rothchild liked by everyone,
I'm married to my love Alecia will never defy her,
And I'm getting old while I'm waiting
   to see the Messiah.

# The Angel

There are trucks and cars,
Honky tonk, clubs and bars,
Angels on high and some fallen,
Few are chosen when God come calling.

One morning, at a McDonald's
I was quaking
I saw a Seraphim in a car taken,
Looking down a crosswalk with
No wings
A favor above all other things.

Years later, my God fearing self,
With much love and scholars wealth
Saw a portrait more than a thousand years old,
As visitations in the Bible foretold.

I was homeless in 1997
And witness to the secret agent
Of Heaven,
Driving through a Spiritual combat zone
In dull primer, glass, metal and
Shining chrome.

The message was, I was made to be aware,
That to even this wretch, God cared
His protection by the Holy Host,
Saved my life from Coast to Coast.

# Final Testimony

It was late in 2019
My body full of funk
At almost 58,
I was rarely clean.

We'd sent out Christmas greetings,
Heard back from Great and small
I had been putting off a doctor's meeting,
When I quit begging and stood tall.

I will always remember,
For the rest of my life,
the odd bruise on my hand in the last December,
All I can think of is the welfare of my Wife.

It's probably nothing,
I quickly rationalized
My angel wife with no ring,
Our love was perfect I realized.

My duty to her, God and Country
That I have to stay one more year
And get back to living healthy,
For them I would cut back on the Smoking and beer.

At home in the Highlands,
At home in the Gulf Stream.
To be the best husband, I am striving.
This morning I awoke from a beautiful dream.

Never made a lot of money
You can be sure of that,
And my final Testimony,
That I wore a white hat.

# Haiku

She died yesterday
My whole life reason, now gone
Today, I will rest.

Years ago my youth
Limo and hotel mostly
I'm old no money

Cold day on the street,
Shelter open for the night
For sleep, no police

# Old Times Rocknroll Rhymes

It was the 21st century
Toboggans blackberry pies and Miller beer,
Dillinger's tommy guns and past crimes
Providence, meds, counseling made for a good year.

That was 20 years ago and it's all changed,
Politically correct snowflakes in Congress,
But I'm not nearly as poor or deranged.
before I found the VA and Jesus I was homeless.

I've had my head up my butt all week,
my uncle told me not to get Medicare,
because the VA gave me a life not so bleak,
A second opinion I thought would be fair.

Jesus and the help of the VA,
Give me health cash and the new wife.
That's why I love, that's why I stay.
But a second opinion might save my life.

Old Times rock and roll rhymes,
Things we never imagined truly die,
So many friends so little time
22 years after Sarge's death, I cried.

# Blue Crab

Me, my mom and dad,
Left our State of Florida Blue Crab,
Because we hated laws of Jim Crowe,
    headed for Ambition, college, jobs
In the Snow.

We lived in the woods near the City,
In the Hudson valley, it's real pretty.
Kipling said that never the Twain shall meet,
The South and the North, the forest
And the Street.

We moved a lot for many years,
Success and mistakes, divorce and tears,
We were transplants and I was run oft,
Out West, I married, my soul aloft.

When I was in the Army in '85,
My Seargent said you have to stand
    and fight to stay alive.
Now on this desert spit of land,
Here God and my wife and I make our stand.

# Rapnroll 2020

Stoney
Was on his owny,
When he met Johnson,
And heard her sad song.

Stoney shows up for Witt,
Baby is the ultimate.
Johnson show up for Stoney,
Brother walk away lonely.

Mother floats above the Storm,
In the light's warmth.
Stoney in a big town,
Stoney shows up for Tucson.

Big kids and little kids,
Stoney and Witt beyond the skins
The Sky and the Sea belong to the Clan,
Rocky Mountains and Volcanic sand.

# Ra and the Snow Moon Pack

Man, Wolf, Sun and Moon,
Farmers, hunters, smoke and food
Valleys, sky and the Winter
National conscience set akilter.

During the rule of King Raa,
Under the moon were born two Alpha
Bright and strong leader pups
In the Last Grass Round Up.

The She-wolf out did a Man trap,
So the pack would have no mishap,
When the herd came to St. John's,
The herd was quickly set upon.

The pickins were plenty,
More than enough for many,
Snow Moon, blood red and Cold,
The hunters got fat and bold.

Nonetheless, Many men persevere,
In the mountains with weather severe,
Smoke and drink from a cup,
Many wolves lost their pups.

Saving the last Alpha, died many,
Raa rule sky and valley,
A herd of deer feasted within the fence,
The loss of crops vast, immense.

In the light of King Raa,
And the subversion of the law,
My ancestors took little and died.
A Brave, cross-legged smoking, sighed.

# Five Meaningful Haikus Valentine's 2020

On Valentine's Day,
We'll eat shrimp and barbeque,
At home in the Sun.

At home, there's much love,
We'll drink a little champagne,
Getting giddy, too.

On Valentine's Day,
We'll wear our new golden rings,
She is number one.

We'll watch a good flick,
Valentine's we stay up late,
We pray, embrace, kiss.

Then it's time for bed,
On our seventh Valentine's,
Each holds the other.

# Double Down on St. John's

Eagle and hawk soar
Seems porpoise frolic and play
Florida today

Drain the DC Swamp
Not the Florida green glades
Progress good for some

St. John's sleep river
And St John's Arizona
Zuni Ranger Braves

Flat hulled river boat
Ancient mountains they beckon
Preserve I reckon

# Here and Now in Tucson

Monsoon so blessed
Ra of the sun rules the land
Campers in a wash

The poor sadly fight
The sun burning very hot
City: nature's guest

Food stamps in the camp
Proud dying men in the ditch
Moving up forward

# The Best in the West
# Time Tripper

Years ago in the Capital City,
Goodness begat envy and it wasn't pretty
We were using hard work and intellect,
When hard times for me began to connect.

I was an unwanted man for all to see,
Alone, cold, no nation or harmony,
But I never gave up my fight
And living alone traveling often at night.

The afternoon anti hero was a born again
I got everything but a blue heaven,
So my life came apart at the seams,
Night terrors and nocturnal scream.

One day in a foreign land,
Where listened to Hagar and the band,
I learned the wisdom of the survivors,
As bare as the cause of Lady Godiva.

In the lands far to the South,
Sage accounts by word of mouth,
I needed right good cover, plain to me,
In the high plateau time travel was meant to be.

Seven paths to Sunday and 21 to a new moon,
Going back and forth, I used a metal spoon,
With fire and Rose, it all coalesced,
I believed I was the best in the West.

Time travel, so hard to say,
A metaphysical premise far astray.
The Grey's whisper and talk,
Priests and scientist often balked.

Whatever the form of your God
   of your understanding,
None of what happened next
   wasn't what I was planning,
I chose to pay it and put my left foot forward,
Years later I move with love's purpose towards,
A NEW LIFE…

Of a golden Palomino I did dream,
In my nightly show low stream s
Prosperous awesome good luck,
Between heaven and hell I was stuck.

Now I have been clean 7 years.
Yes, I smoke State Weed and drink beer,
Coffee in the morning with my Lady Fair,
Keeping her happy is my biggest affair.

We've been married years number four,
I gave up my bad habit of days of yore,
Surely He has blessed me with His Word,
I love Alecia beyond heaven and Earth.

# About the Authors

Mark Fleming Stonesifer is a totally and permanently disabled veteran who served in both the US Army and US Navy from 1984 to 1994. Mark graduated from the College of General Studies at Boston Univers ity in 1982. He graduated from Regents College with a Bachelor of Science degree while on active duty in the US Navy in 1990 and has lived in Latin America.

Alecia Zoe Witt Stonesifer has lived in Europe, worked for many years in the Club and Hotel industry and as a commercial baker. She's the mother of four adult children and while in school she was a member of the National Honor Society and Chorus as well as active in team sports.

The Stonesifers were married after a two year engagement. They both have happy memories of scouting in the Hudson River valley, as well as Texas and Arizona. They promote Christian values in their home.

Lightning Source UK Ltd.
Milton Keynes UK
UKHW021851200520
363522UK00010B/227